Everyday Materials

Glass

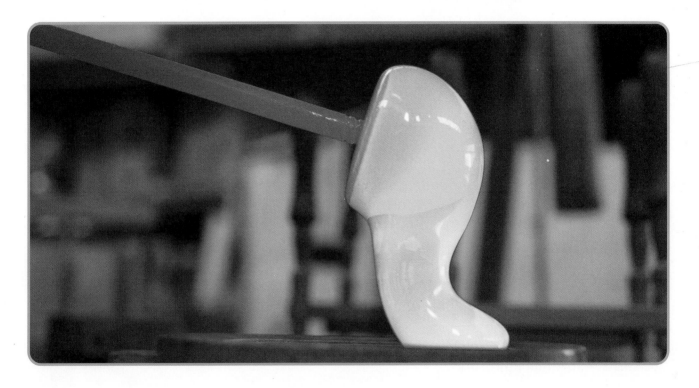

Andrew Langley

WAYLAND

First published in 2008
by Wayland

Wayland
338 Euston Road
London NW1 3BH

Wayland Australia
Level 17/207 Kent Street
Sydney, NSW 2000

Editor: Annabel Savery
Designer: Ian Winton
Illustrator: Ian Winton
Picture researcher: Rachel Tisdale

Acknowledgements: Corbis: Cover main (Arcaid/Peter Durant), title page, 12 and 21 (Martin Ruetschi / Keystone), 7 (Paul A Souders), 10 (Bob Krist), 11 and 19 (James L Amos). Discovery Picture Library: 16, 18. Department of Defense: 15. IstockPhoto: cover and spread head panel (Rolf Klebsattel), 4 (Oktay Ortakcioglu), 5 (Milos Luzanin), 6 (Francis Twitty), 9 (Tom Young), 13 (Emily Engler), 14, 19 (Tracy Hebden), 20 (Robert Hillman). Nasa: 17. Pilkington Glass: 8.

British Library Cataloguing in Publication Data
Langley, Andrew
   Glass. – (Everyday materials)
   1. Glass – Juvenile literature
   I. Title
   620.1'44

ISBN: 978 0 75025 321 5

Printed in China

Wayland is a division of Hachette Children's Books,
an Hachette Livre UK company.

Contents

What is glass?

Glass is a material you can see
through. It is strong and hard,
but it can also break very easily.

Glass is made mostly from sand. It can be shaped into thousands of different things, including windows, bottles and light bulbs.

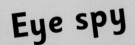

Eye spy

Look around your classroom. How many glass objects can you see?

5

How is glass made?

Sand is crushed into powder. Then it is mixed with other materials, such as **limestone** and **sodium**.

The mixture is put into a big tank. This goes into a **furnace** where it gets very hot. The sand mixture melts and turns into runny glass.

Flat glass

Molten glass is made into many different shapes. It can be spread out on a layer of hot metal. The hot metal makes the glass flat and smooth.

Did you know?

The flat sheets of glass are moved on huge rollers.

Molten glass floating on a layer of hot metal.

When it cools, the glass becomes hard again. It is lifted from the metal. The big sheet is cut into smaller pieces.

Flat glass can be used to make big windows.

Blowing

A glass-blower shapes glass by blowing air into it. He dips a long hollow pipe into molten glass.

Then he blows air through the pipe into the molten glass to make the shape.

The air makes the glass bulge out into a round bulb shape.

Did you know?

There are glass-blowing machines which make glass bottles.

Casting and pressing

Glass can be shaped by pouring it into a **mould**. When the glass cools, it is in the shape of the mould. This is called casting.

Eye spy

Can you see anyone wearing glasses? The **lenses** in glasses are made by casting.

12

Machines also press glass into shapes. A piece of molten glass is dropped into a mould. A **plunger** presses it down to fill the shape of the mould. This is called pressing.

The lens in a camera is made by pressing.

Glass fibre

Molten glass can be squeezed
through tiny holes. It
comes out in very
thin threads
called **fibres**.
The threads are
woven into a
material called
fibreglass.

Did you know?

Special glass fibres can carry light. Some fibres can even carry telephone and TV signals.

14

Fibreglass is very strong. It will not burn. Fibreglass is used to make boats, and clothing for fire fighters.

Special uses

A mirror is a sheet of glass with a layer of shiny metal on one side. It **reflects** light.

Look into a mirror. You will see your own face in it. This is the light from your face being reflected back to you.

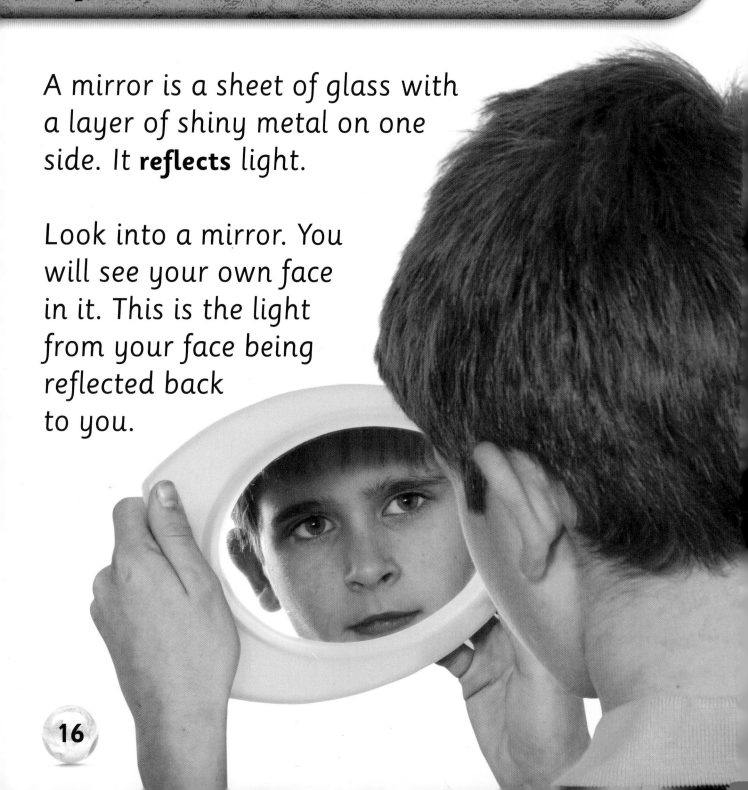

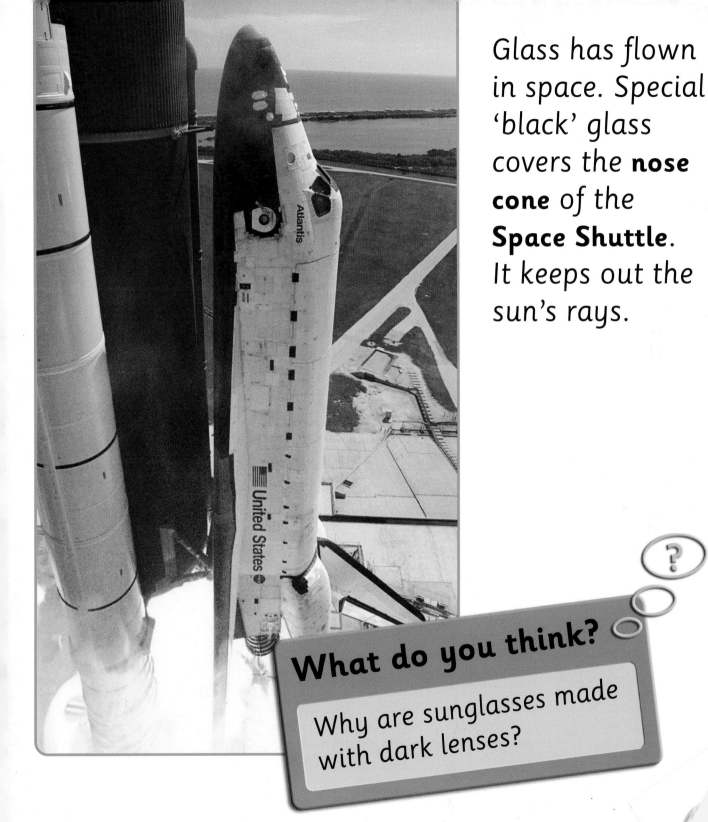

Glass has flown in space. Special 'black' glass covers the **nose cone** of the **Space Shuttle**. It keeps out the sun's rays.

What do you think?

Why are sunglasses made with dark lenses?

Recycling

It takes a lot of energy to make new glass. But old glass is easier to melt down and use again.

Eye spy

Does your family have a recycling box for empty glass bottles and jars?

Glass-makers add waste glass to sand when they make new glass. It helps the sand to melt more quickly.

Waste glass is collected and crushed ready to be used again.

Quiz

Questions

1. What is the main material used for making glass?
2. What happens when molten glass cools down?
3. How does a glass-blower make shapes in glass?
4. Can you set fire to fibreglass?
5. Is old glass easy to melt again?

Answers

1. Sand.
2. It gets hard.
3. A glass-blower blows air into the glass so that it forms a round bulb.
4. No – it will not burn.
5. Yes.

Glass topic web

Music
If you blow across the top of a glass bottle you can make a whistling noise. You can change the noise if you put water in the bottle.

Art and design
You can get special paints to paint on glass. You can use them to decorate drinking glasses.

History
The Egyptians were some of the first people to make glass. They made beads out of glass.

Science
Glass lenses can make things look bigger. You can use a **magnifying glass** to look closely at things.

Geography
Obsidian is a type of rock that is just like glass. It is made when the hot rock from a volcano cools down very quickly.

Glossary

fibre a thin strand or thread

furnace a special large oven which is heated by electricity or burning fuel

lens a piece of glass specially moulded so it makes things look bigger

limestone a chalky kind of rock

magnifying glass a glass lens that makes things look bigger

molten when a material has been heated to a very high temperature and becomes a thick liquid

mould a container which is shaped in a special way, a liquid which is poured in will take the same shape

nose cone the front part of a rocket or spacecraft

plunger a metal arm which pushes down objects

reflect to send back something

sodium a soft white chemical (table salt is a kind of sodium)

Space Shuttle an aircraft which can travel into space and back again

Further information

Books to read

Find Out About: Find Out About Glass. Henry Pluckrose. Franklin Watts Ltd, 2002.

Raintree Perspectives: Using Materials: How We Use Glass. Chris Oxlade. Raintree Publishers, 2004.

Start-Up Science: Materials. Claire Llewellyn. Evans Brothers Ltd, 2004.

Web sites to visit

BBC Schools
http://www.bbc.co.uk/schools/scienceclips/ages/5_6/sorting_using_ mate.shtml
Learn all about different types of materials and their properties.

Glass Forever
http://www.glassforever.co.uk/
Here you can learn all about glass. The website has lots of information, as well as games and news stories.

Recycling Guide
http://www.recycling-guide.org.uk/science-glass.html
Learn all about how glass is recycled.

Index